EYEWITNESS ● READERS

Level 2
BEGINNING TO READ ALONE

Bugs! Bugs! Bugs!

Written by Jennifer Dussling

DORLING KINDERSLEY
London • New York • Moscow • Sydney

Stag beetle

Help!

Bugs look scary close up.

But *you* don't need to worry.

Dragonfly

Most bugs are a danger
only to other insects.
They are the bugs
that really bug
other bugs.

*Praying
mantis*

*Weevil-
hunting
wasp*

This praying mantis
sits perfectly still.
But if you are a bug,
watch out!
A fly lands on a branch
near a praying mantis.
The mantis fixes
its big eyes on the fly.

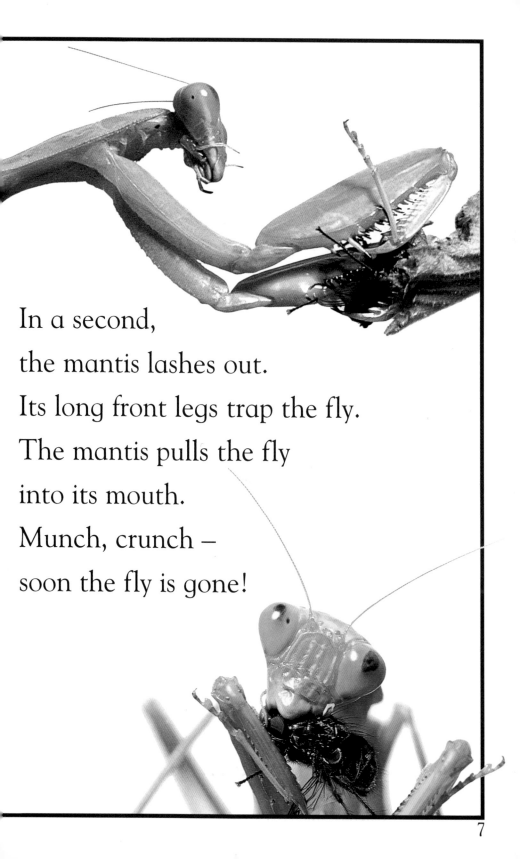

In a second,
the mantis lashes out.
Its long front legs trap the fly.
The mantis pulls the fly
into its mouth.
Munch, crunch –
soon the fly is gone!

Some bugs hunt other bugs,
not to eat themselves,
but to feed to their babies.
This hunting wasp
has just stung a weevil.

Weevil-hunting wasp

It will drag the weevil to its nest and
lay eggs on the weevil.
When the eggs hatch,
the young wasps, called grubs,
will eat up the weevil.

Hairy food

The spider-hunting wasp
catches huge spiders
for its grubs.
Sometimes it takes over
the spider's home, too!

Wood ants are tiny.
But they have sharp jaws and
they can squirt acid
from their bodies.
This acid can kill
another bug.

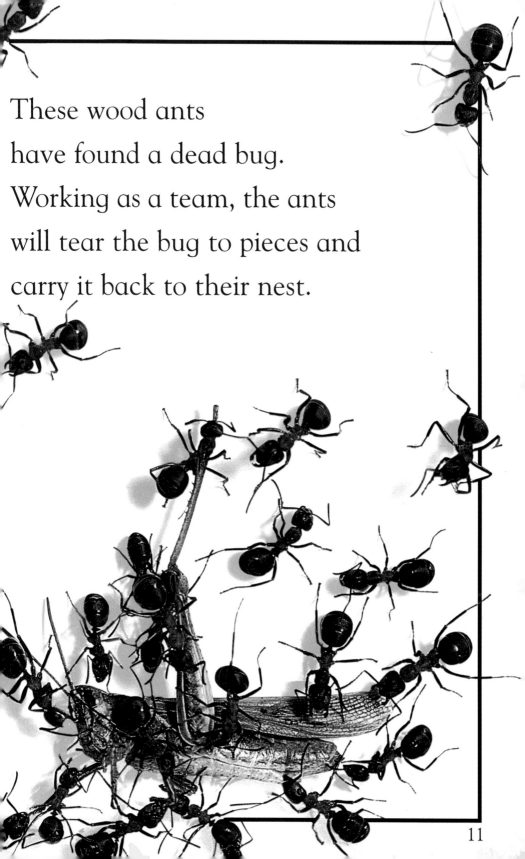

These wood ants
have found a dead bug.
Working as a team, the ants
will tear the bug to pieces and
carry it back to their nest.

It's a quiet day by a pond.
One second, a mosquito
is buzzing along.
The next second,
a dragonfly swoops down and
snaps the mosquito
right out of the air!

Dragonflies are flying killers
that eat and eat and eat.
In half an hour, they can eat
their own body weight.
That's like you eating
250 sandwiches!

Ancient insect
Dragonflies were around
long before the dinosaurs!
This dragonfly rotted away
millions of years ago.
It left its print in a rock.

An assassin is a person who kills
another person on purpose.
The assassin bug is a bug
that really lives up
to its name.

Some assassin bugs
are called kissing bugs.
This is because
they often bite people
on the face.

When it catches another insect,

it injects the insect with poison.

The poison turns

the bug's insides to soup.

Then the assassin bug

sucks up the soup!

Only one bug
has to watch out for
a male stag beetle –
another male stag beetle!
What do they fight about?
Usually a female
stag beetle!

The fighting beetles
poke at each other,
then lock jaws.

One beetle grabs
the other beetle
and throws him.
The loser
scurries away.

*Monarch
butterfly
caterpillar*

With so many killer bugs and
other hungry animals,
how do any insects survive?

Hoverfly

Click beetle

All these bugs have special ways
to trick their enemies.
You can read about them
if you turn the page.

*Postman
butterfly
caterpillar*

Stinkbugs have glands
that make smells.
Some stinkbugs
ooze a nasty-smelling liquid
when they are in danger.
That's a big turn-off!

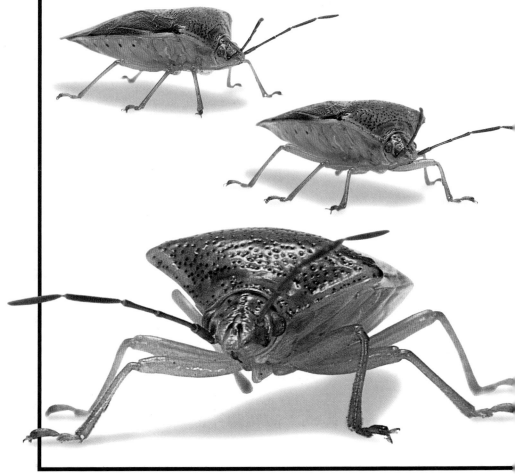

Stinkbugs are also known
as shieldbugs.
Some use their flat bodies
to shield their young
from hungry insects and birds.

The monarch butterfly
looks easy to capture and eat.
But hungry bugs and birds
leave it alone.
Why?

In the insect world,
bright colours are a warning.
Bright orange signals that
this butterfly tastes bad.
Even the monarch caterpillars
taste awful.

Changing faces
When a caterpillar
is fully grown,
it changes into a butterfly
inside a hard case like this,
called a chrysalis (KRISS-uh-liss).

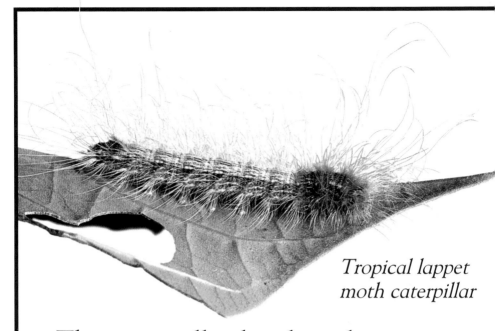

*Tropical lappet
moth caterpillar*

This caterpillar has long hairs
that break easily.
When enemies try to catch it,
they get a mouthful
of hair instead!

Safety in numbers
Caterpillars sometimes
huddle together.
They flick their heads up
to startle a hungry enemy.

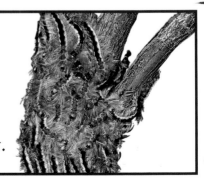

And this spiky caterpillar
can be deadly.
The leaves that it eats
make its body poisonous.
It is not harmed by the poison but
its enemies are!

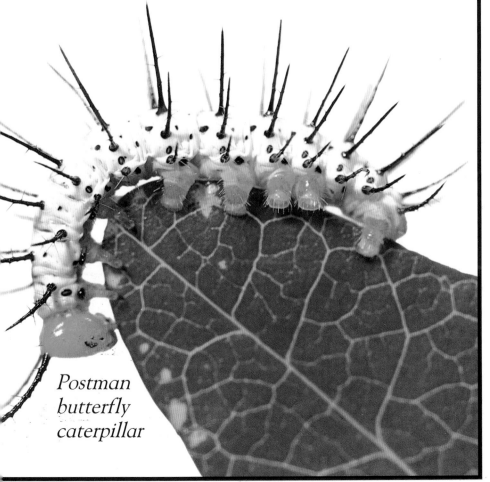

*Postman
butterfly
caterpillar*

A thornbug is good at hiding.
It looks like a thorn on a twig.
A bird looking for a meal
might not see it.

Thornbugs are clever, too.
Sometimes they all face
the same way and
stay very still!

To avoid being eaten,
this click beetle
has a clever way of escaping.

It arches its back and then
jumps into the air.

If the beetle
lands upside down,
it throws itself into the air again –
this time hoping to land safely
on its feet!

Flashing lights

Some click beetles
send out light signals.
These flashing lights
help the beetles
to find a mate.

One of these bugs
is a harmless hoverfly.
The other is a hornet
with a nasty sting.
Can you tell
which is which?
No?

Neither can most bugs and birds!
That's why they leave
both of these insects alone.
Do you still not know which is which?
The fly is the bug
on the left!

Bug Facts

There are at least one million
different kinds of insects
in the world.

Sometimes all insects
are called "bugs".
But the true bugs
are those that have
sharp, straw-like tubes
for feeding.

All insects have six legs,
and most have wings
at some time in their lives.

Some insects hear with their legs.
Other insects taste with their feet.

A few insects eat and eat
when they are young.
But when they get older,
they don't eat anything at all.

Some bugs have amazing vision and
can see colours
that people cannot see.